This Journal Belongs To

"Let all that you do be done in love."

1 Corinthians 16:14

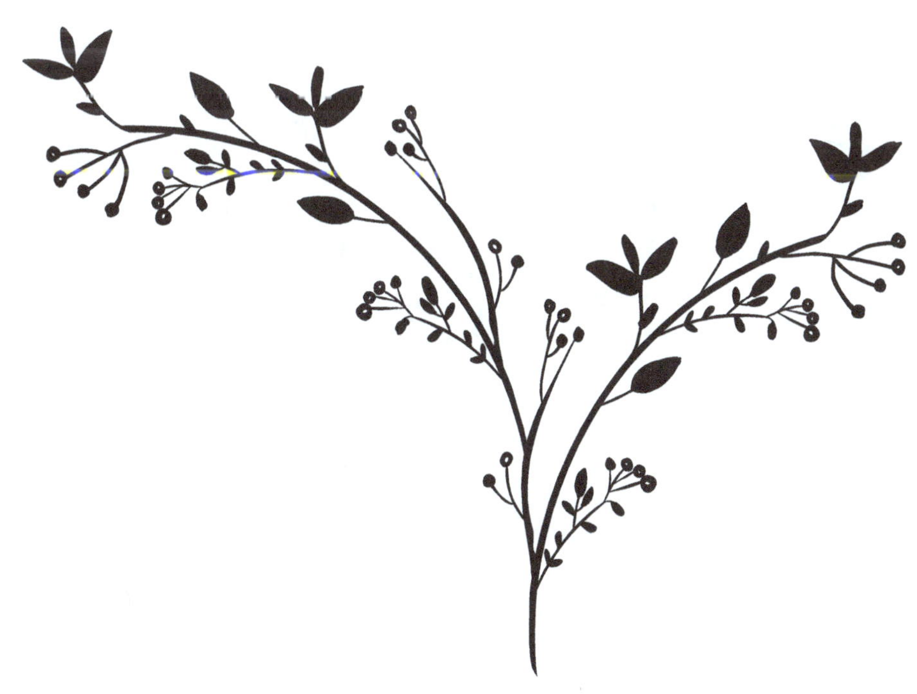

Please note: Blank pages protect your artwork from bleed through. However, these pages can be used for drawings or whatever expression is on your heart.

Enjoy!

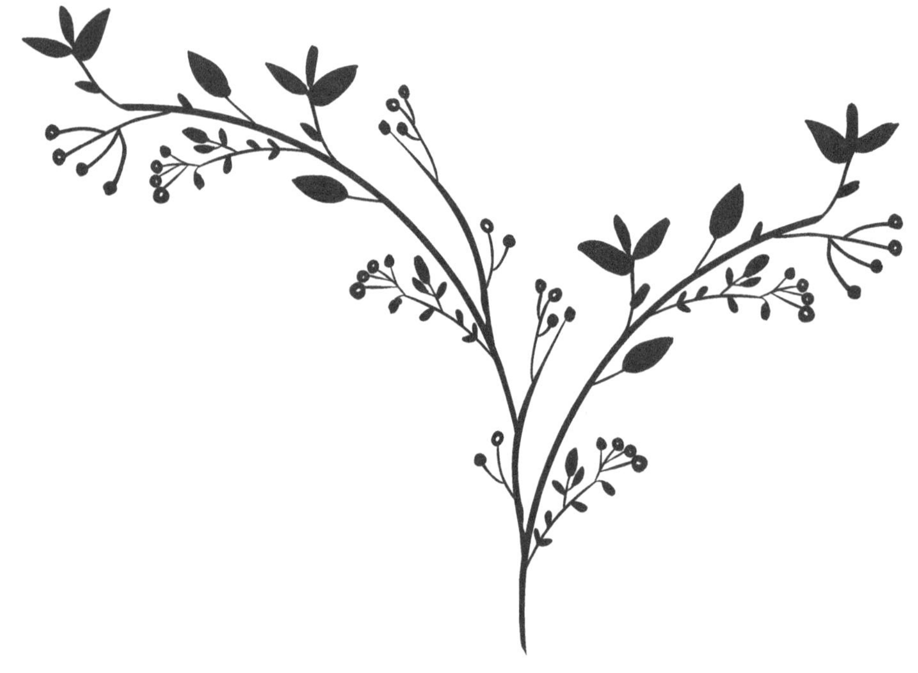

KING OF KINGS!

KING OF KINGS!

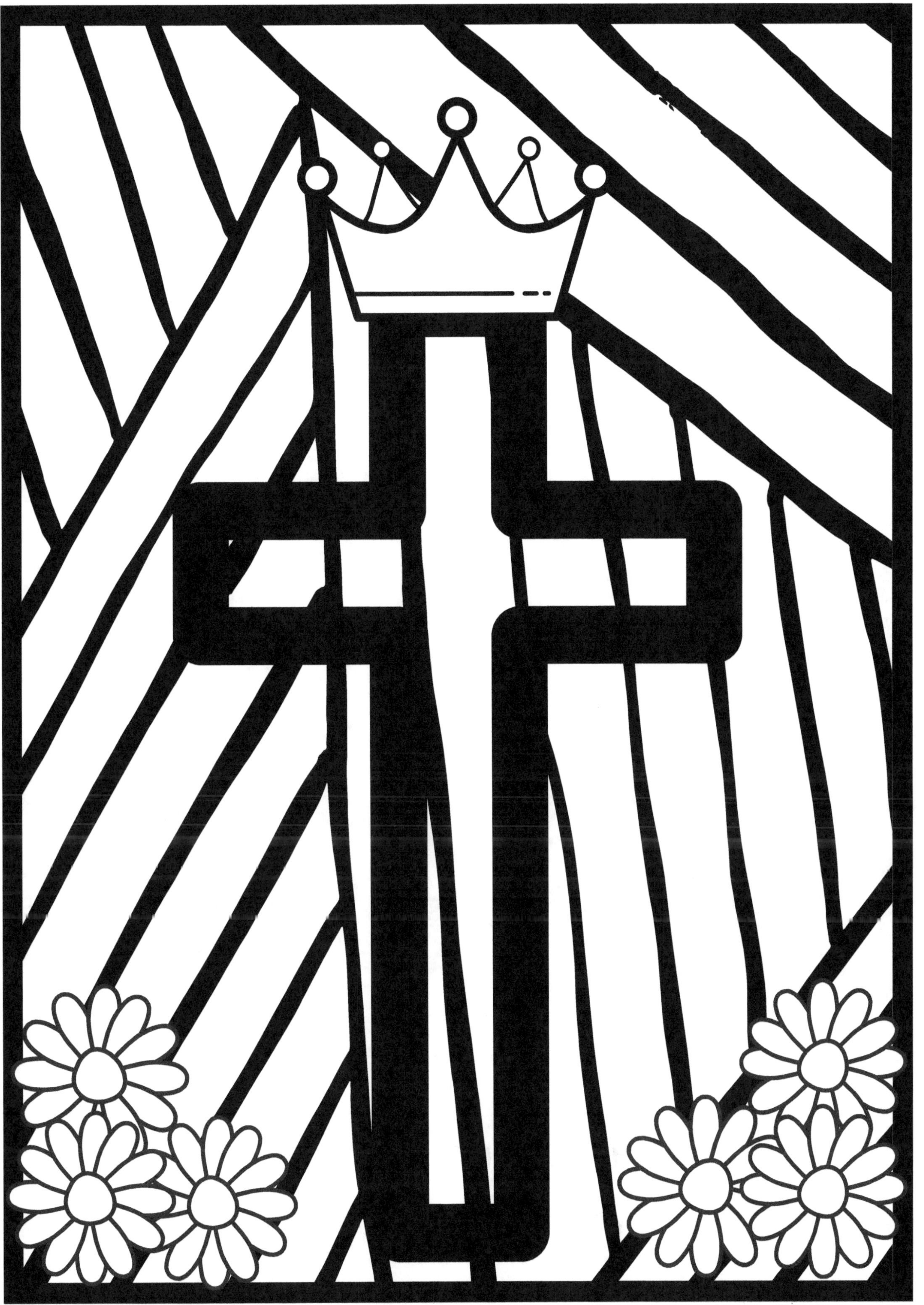

""Let all that you do be done in love."

1 Corinthians 16:14

PRAISE HIM!

PRAISE HIM!

I WILL BLESS THE LORD AT ALL TIMES;

HIS PRAISE SHALL CONTINUALLY BE IN MY MOUTH

Psalm 34:1-4

""Let all that you do be done in love."

1 Corinthians 16:14

HAVE FAITH!

HAVE FAITH!

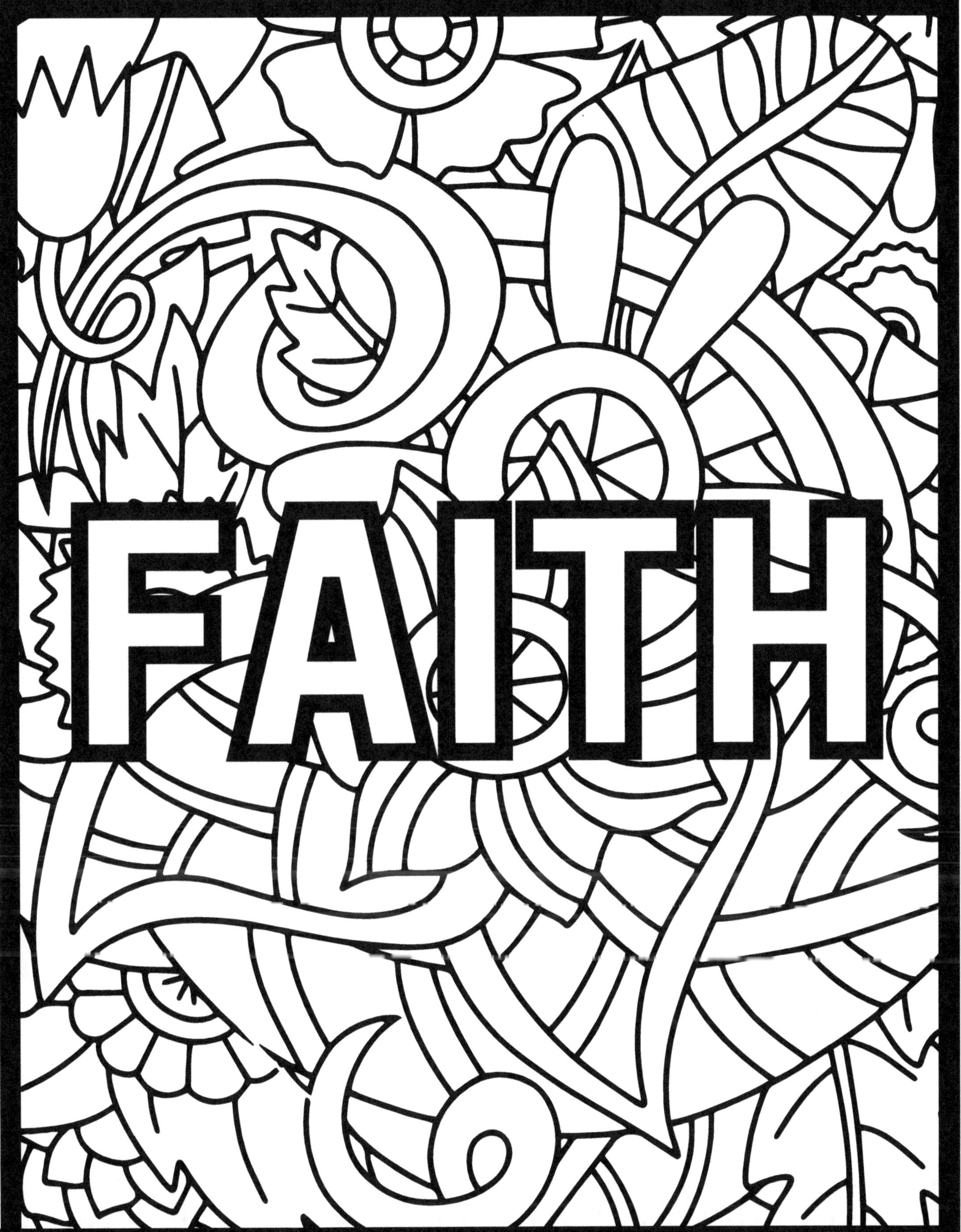

Three things will last forever—faith, hope, and love—and the greatest of these is love. 1 Corinthians 13:13

""Let all that you do be done in love."
1 Corinthians 16:14

JESUS PAID IT ALL!

JESUS PAID IT ALL!

JESUS
PAID
IT
ALL

""Let all that you do be done in love."
1 Corinthians 16:14

YOU CAN DO IT!

YOU CAN DO IT!

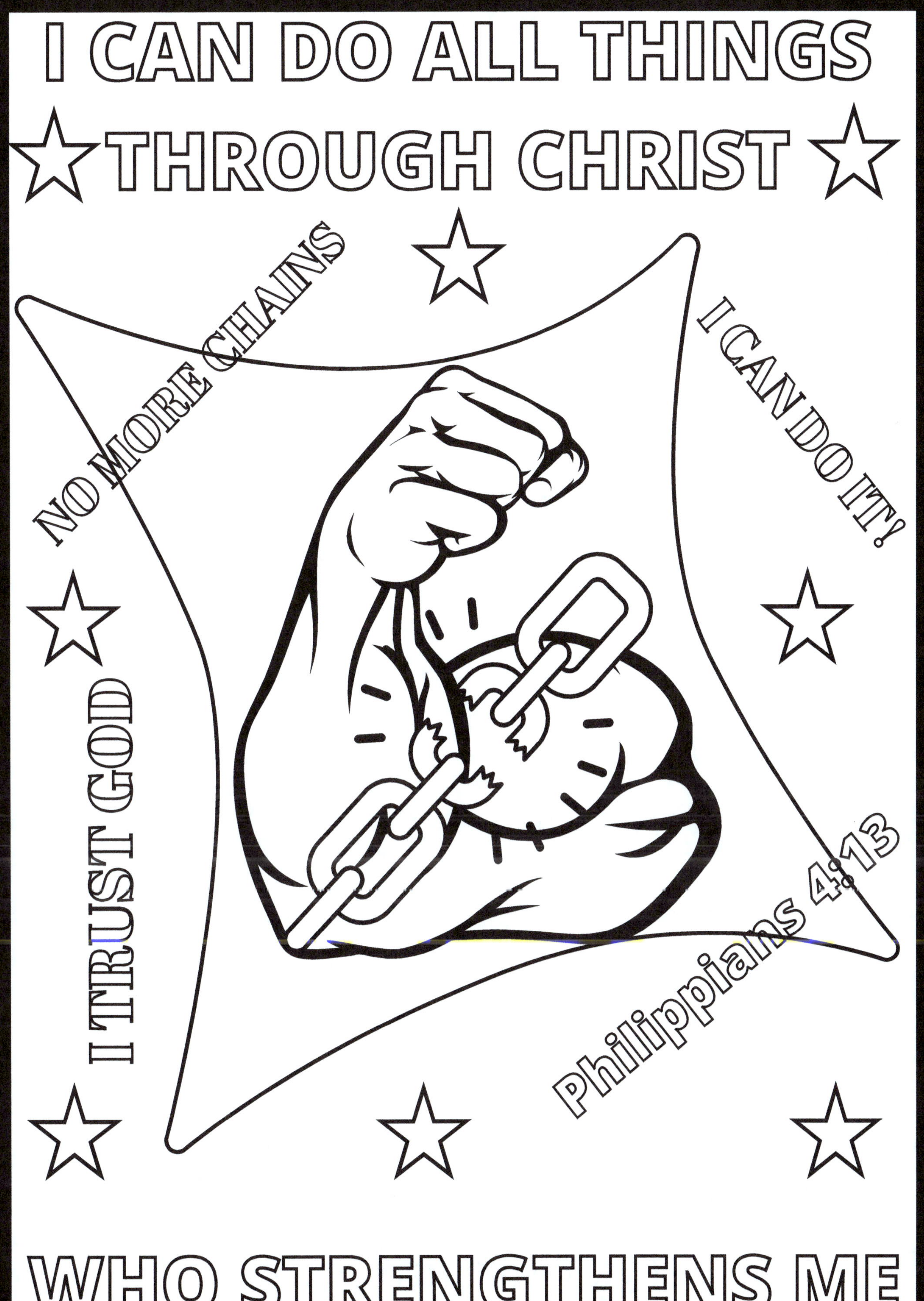

I CAN DO ALL THINGS
THROUGH CHRIST
NO MORE CHAINS
I CAN DO IT!
I TRUST GOD
Philippians 4:13
WHO STRENGTHENS ME

""Let all that you do be done in love."
1 Corinthians 16:14

YOU'RE BLESSED!

YOU'RE BLESSED!

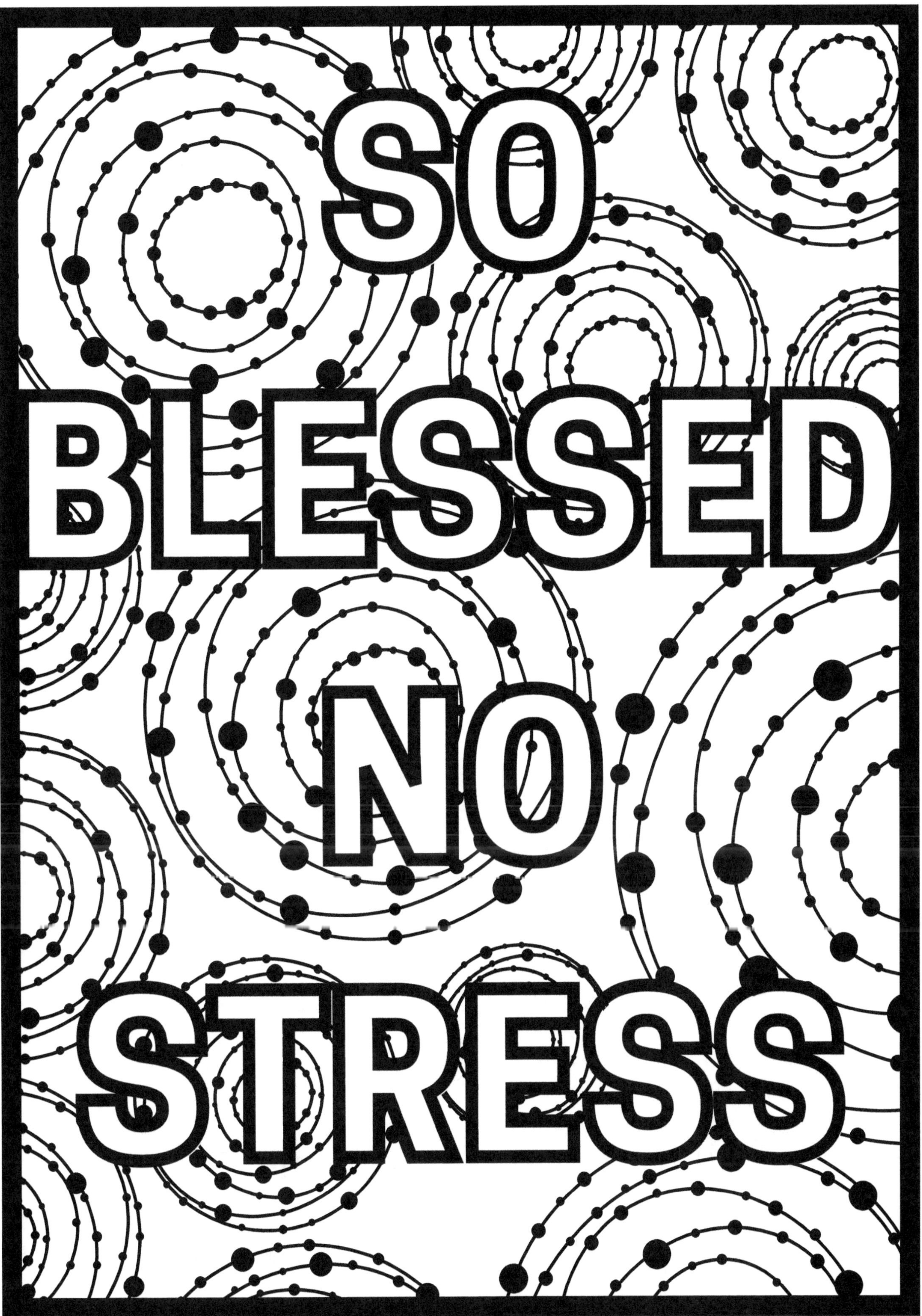
SO
BLESSED
NO
STRESS

""Let all that you do be done in love."

1 Corinthians 16:14

BELIEVE!

BELIEVE!

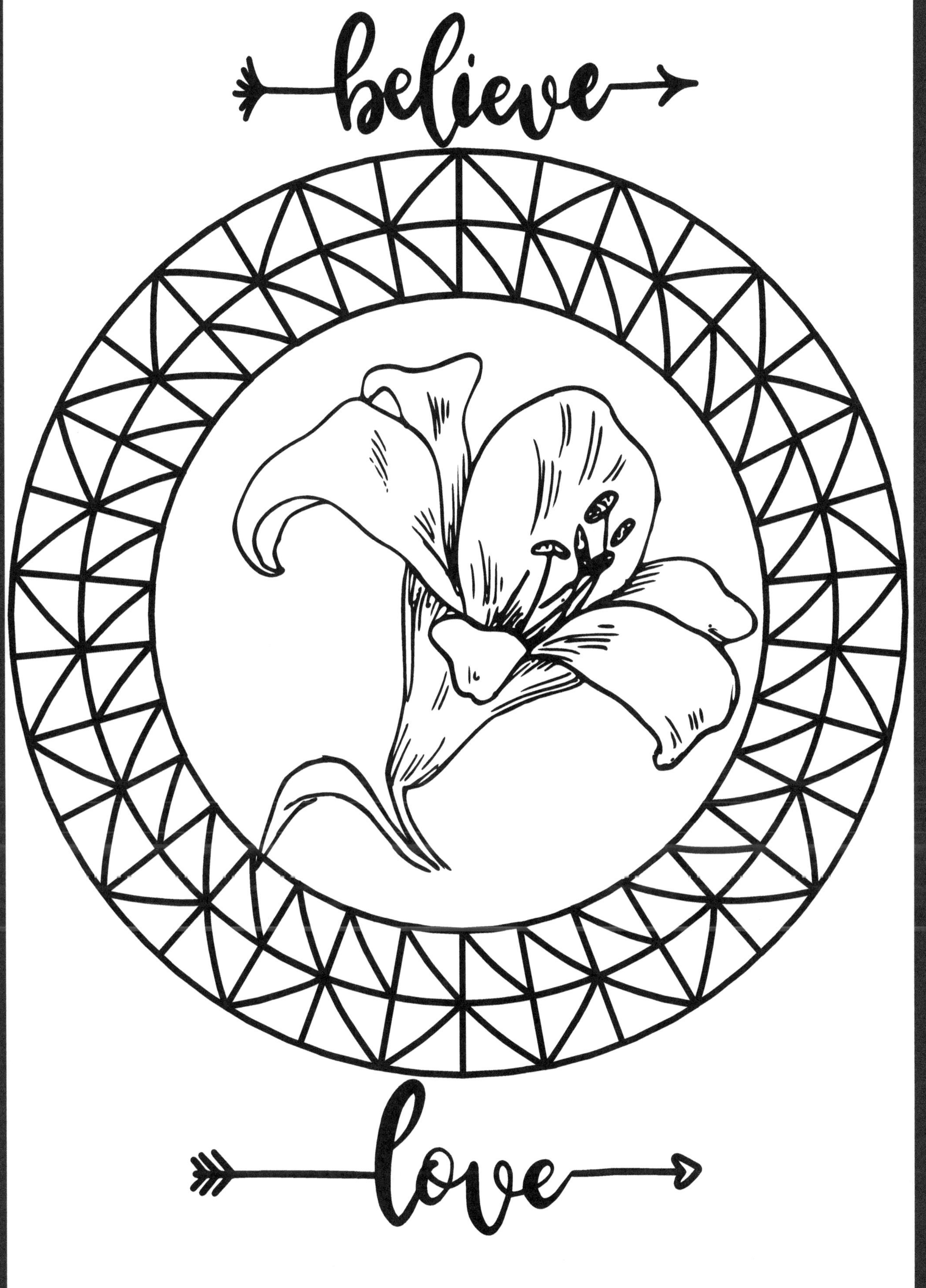
believe
love

""Let all that you do be done in love."

1 Corinthians 16:14

THANK YOU LORD!

THANK YOU LORD!

"O GIVE THANKS UNTO THE LORD; FOR HE IS GOOD: FOR HIS MERCY ENDURETH FOREVER."

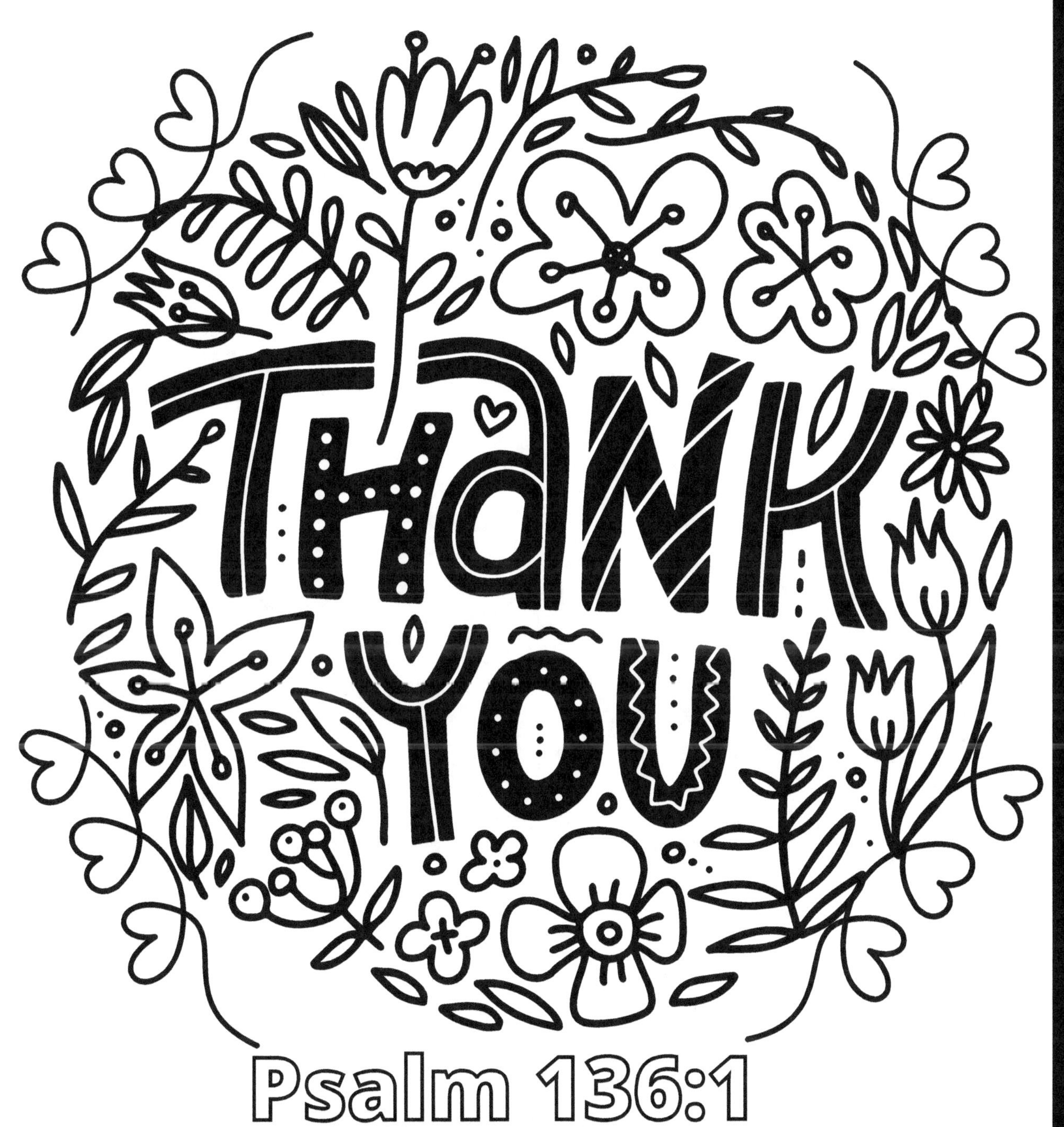

Psalm 136:1

""Let all that you do be done in love."

1 Corinthians 16:14

THERE'S POWER IN THE NAME OF JESUS!

THERE'S POWER IN THE NAME OF JESUS!

JESUS
JESUS
JESUS
JESUS

""Let all that you do be done in love."

1 Corinthians 16:14

YOU ARE FORGIVEN!

YOU ARE FORGIVEN!

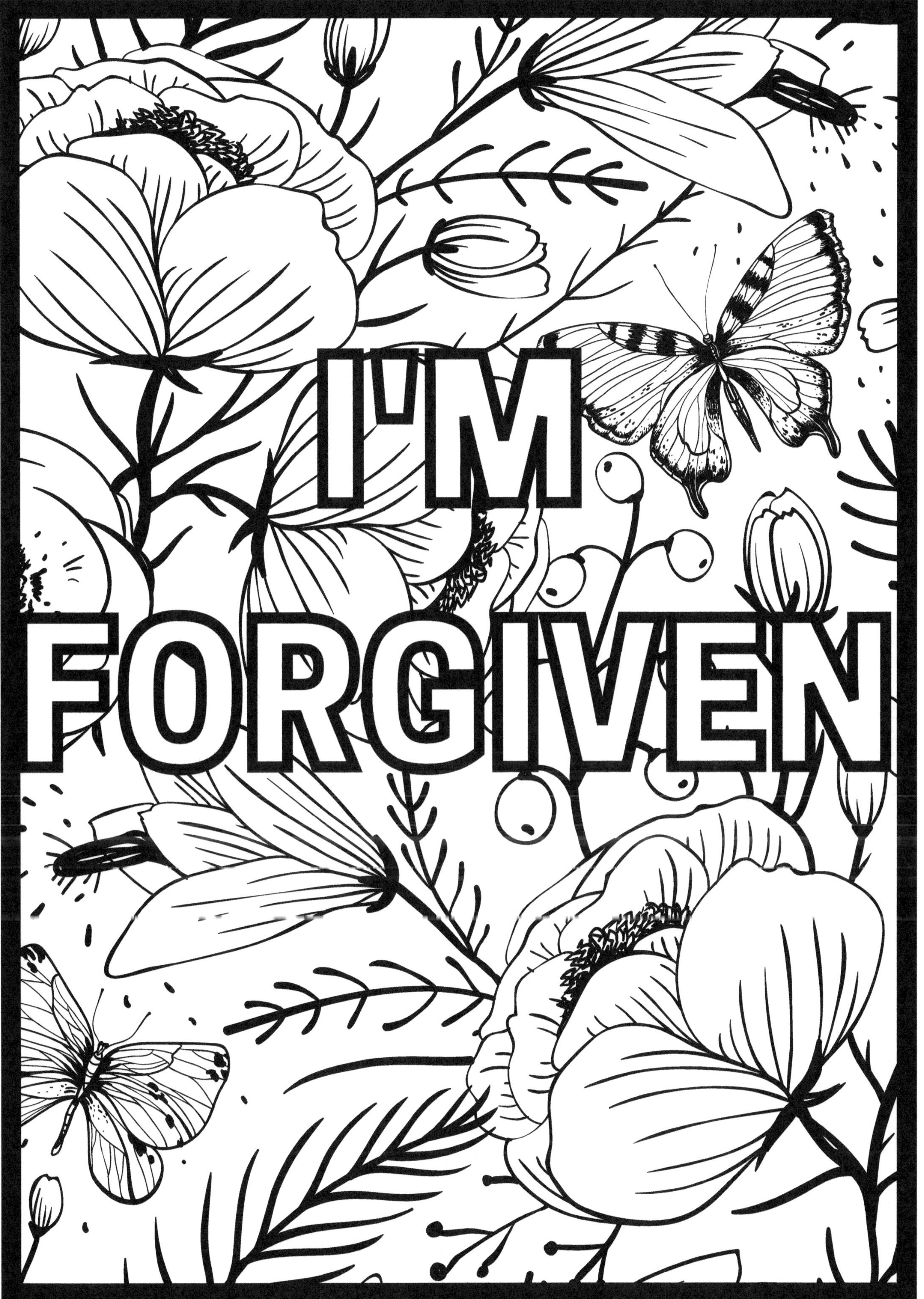
I'M
FORGIVEN

""Let all that you do be done in love."

1 Corinthians 16:14

PROTECTOR!

PROTECTOR!

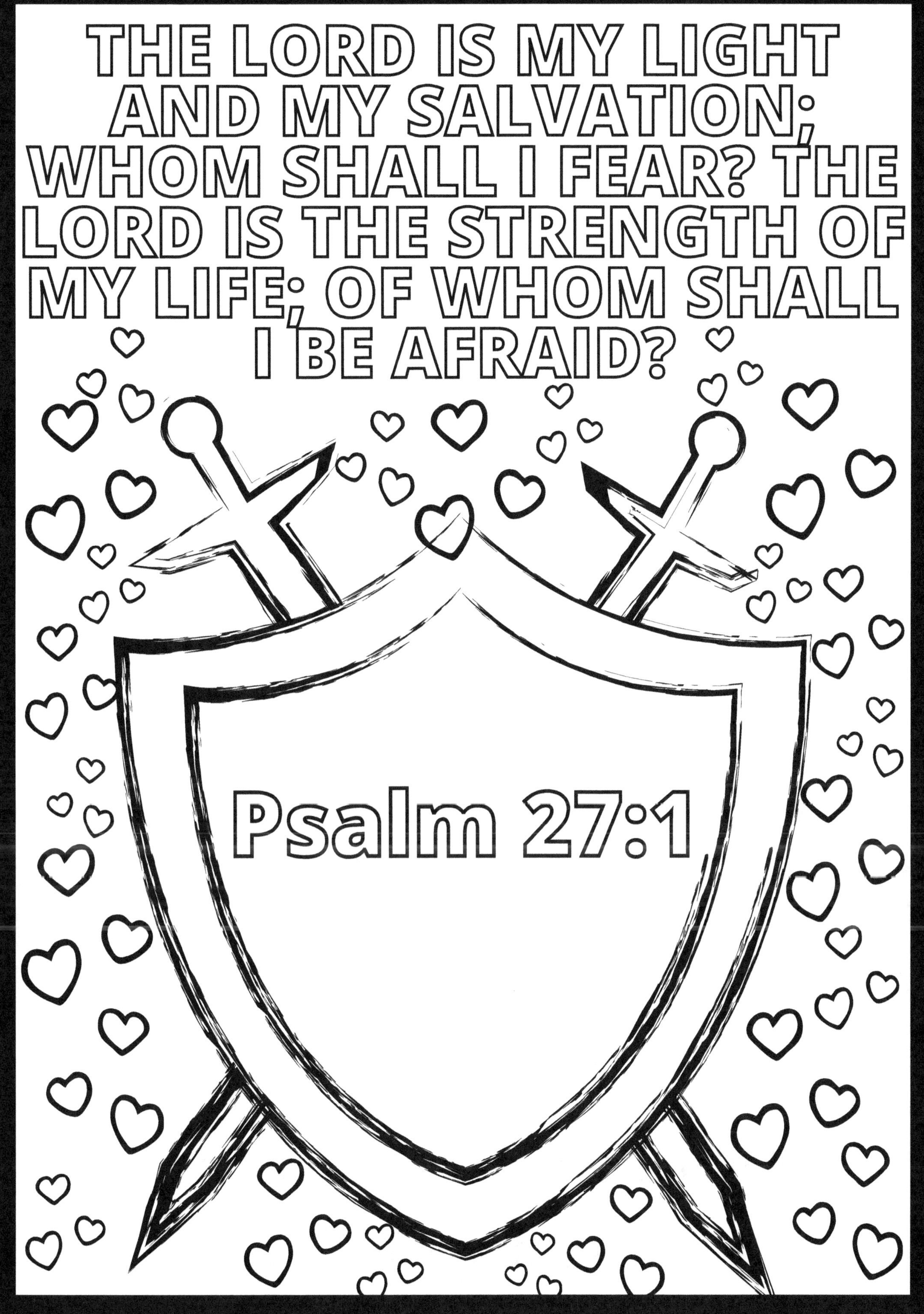
THE LORD IS MY LIGHT
AND MY SALVATION;
WHOM SHALL I FEAR? THE
LORD IS THE STRENGTH OF
MY LIFE; OF WHOM SHALL
I BE AFRAID?
Psalm 27:1

""Let all that you do be done in love."

1 Corinthians 16:14

WORSHIP!

WORSHIP!

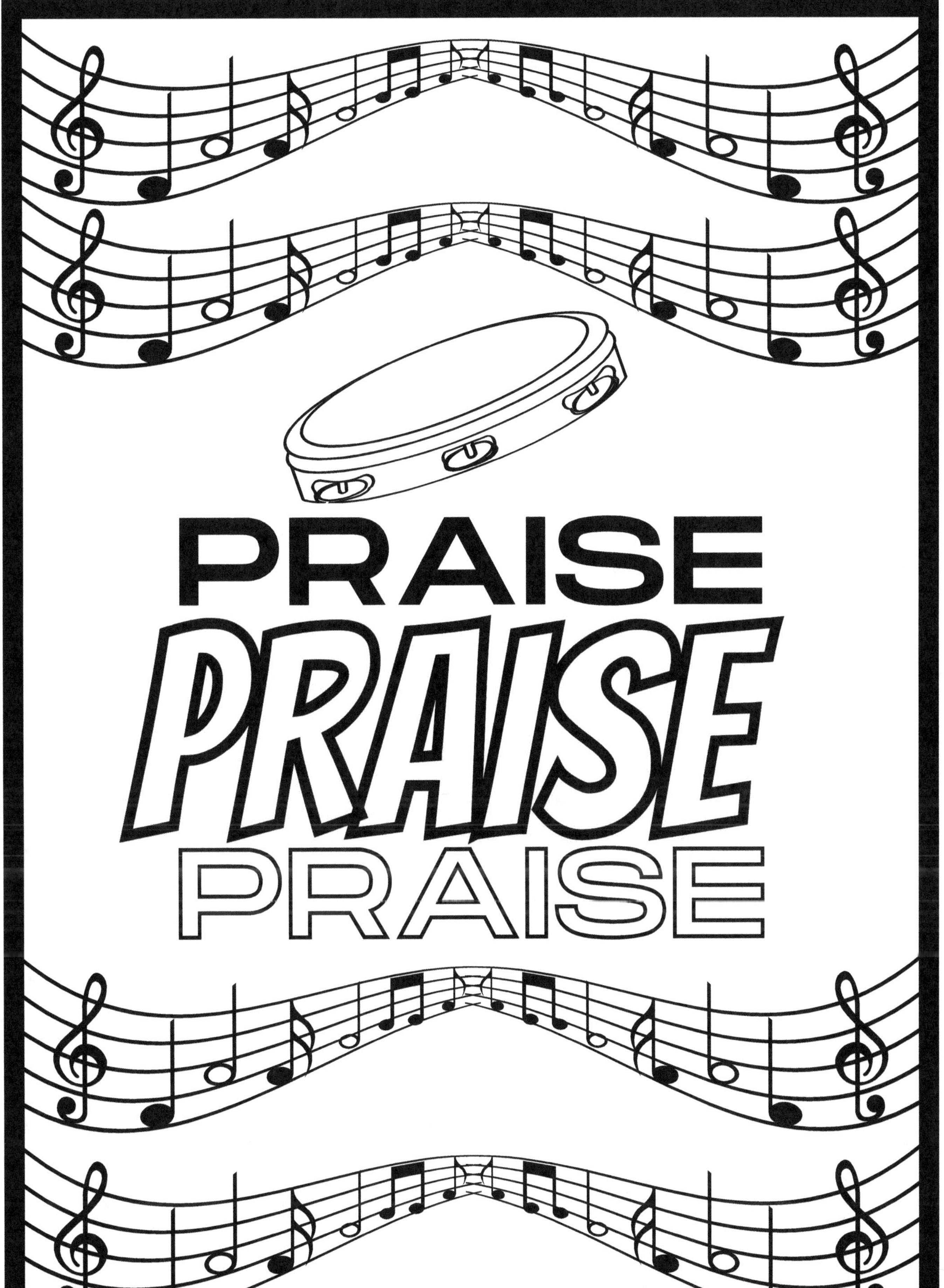
PRAISE
PRAISE
PRAISE

""Let all that you do be done in love."

1 Corinthians 16:14

GOD LOVES YOU!

GOD LOVES YOU!

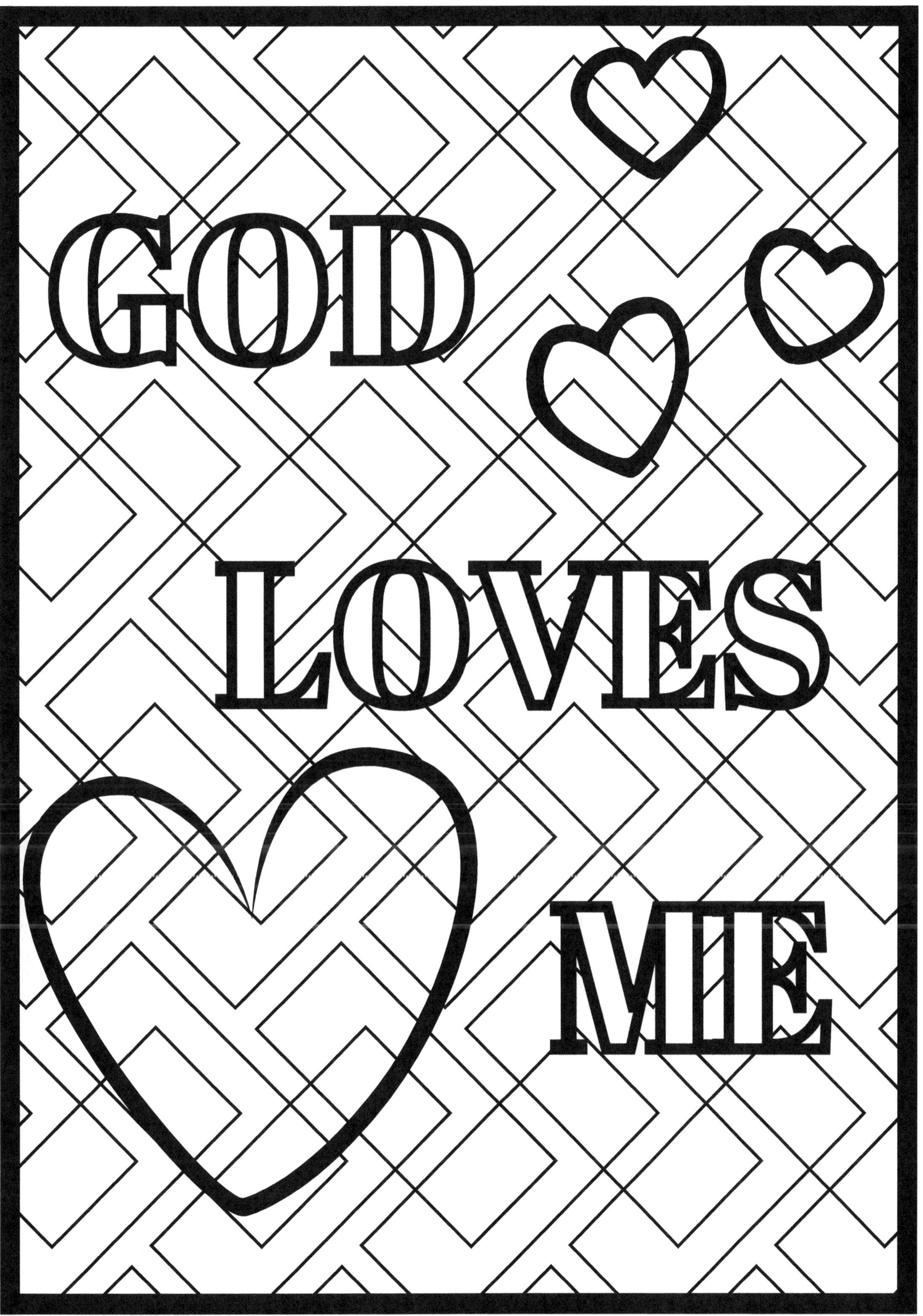
GOD
LOVES
ME

""Let all that you do be done in love."
1 Corinthians 16:14

THE WORD OF GOD!

THE WORD OF GOD!

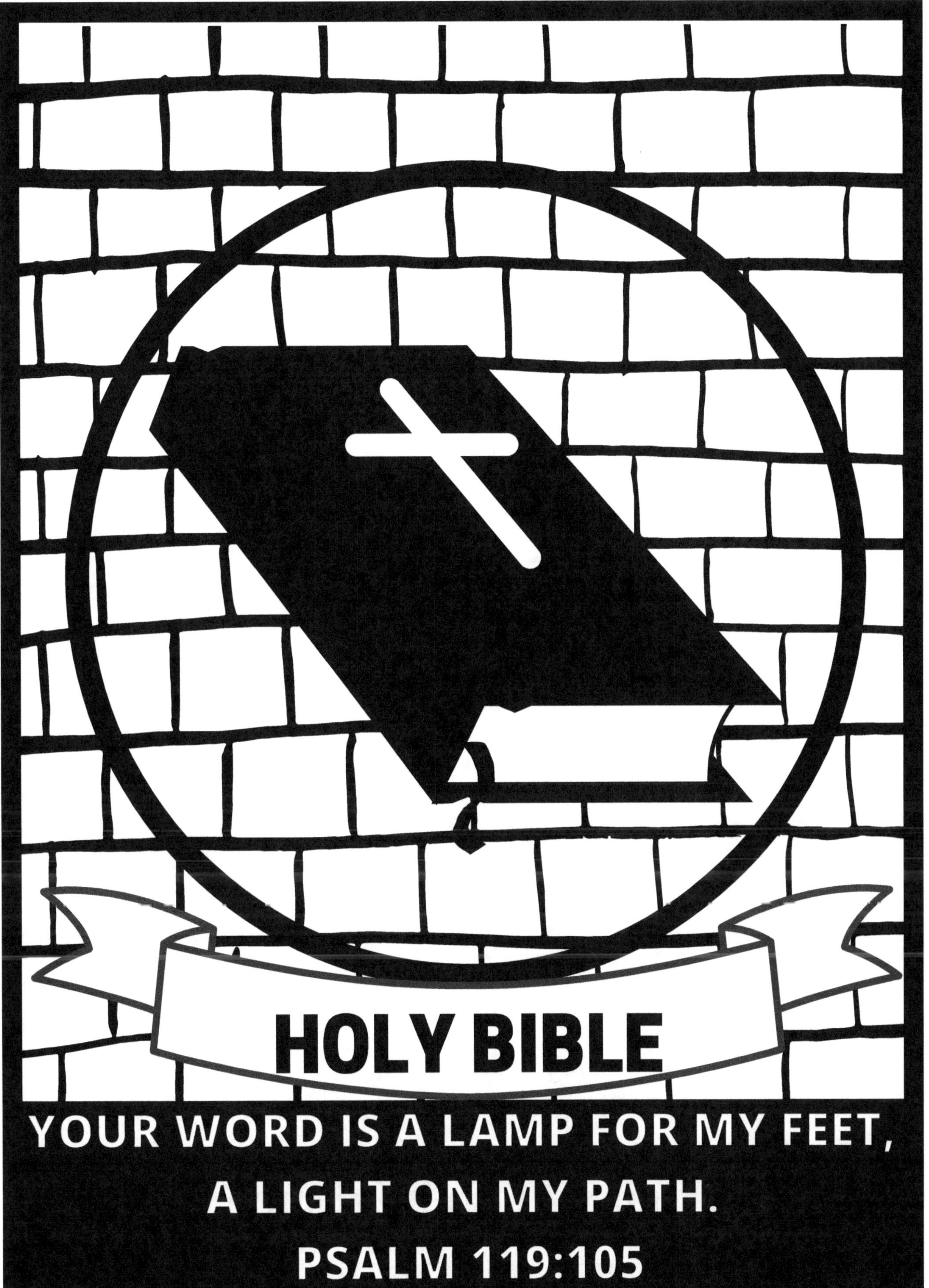
HOLY BIBLE
YOUR WORD IS A LAMP FOR MY FEET,
A LIGHT ON MY PATH.
PSALM 119:105

""Let all that you do be done in love."

1 Corinthians 16:14

THERE'S HOPE!

THERE'S HOPE!

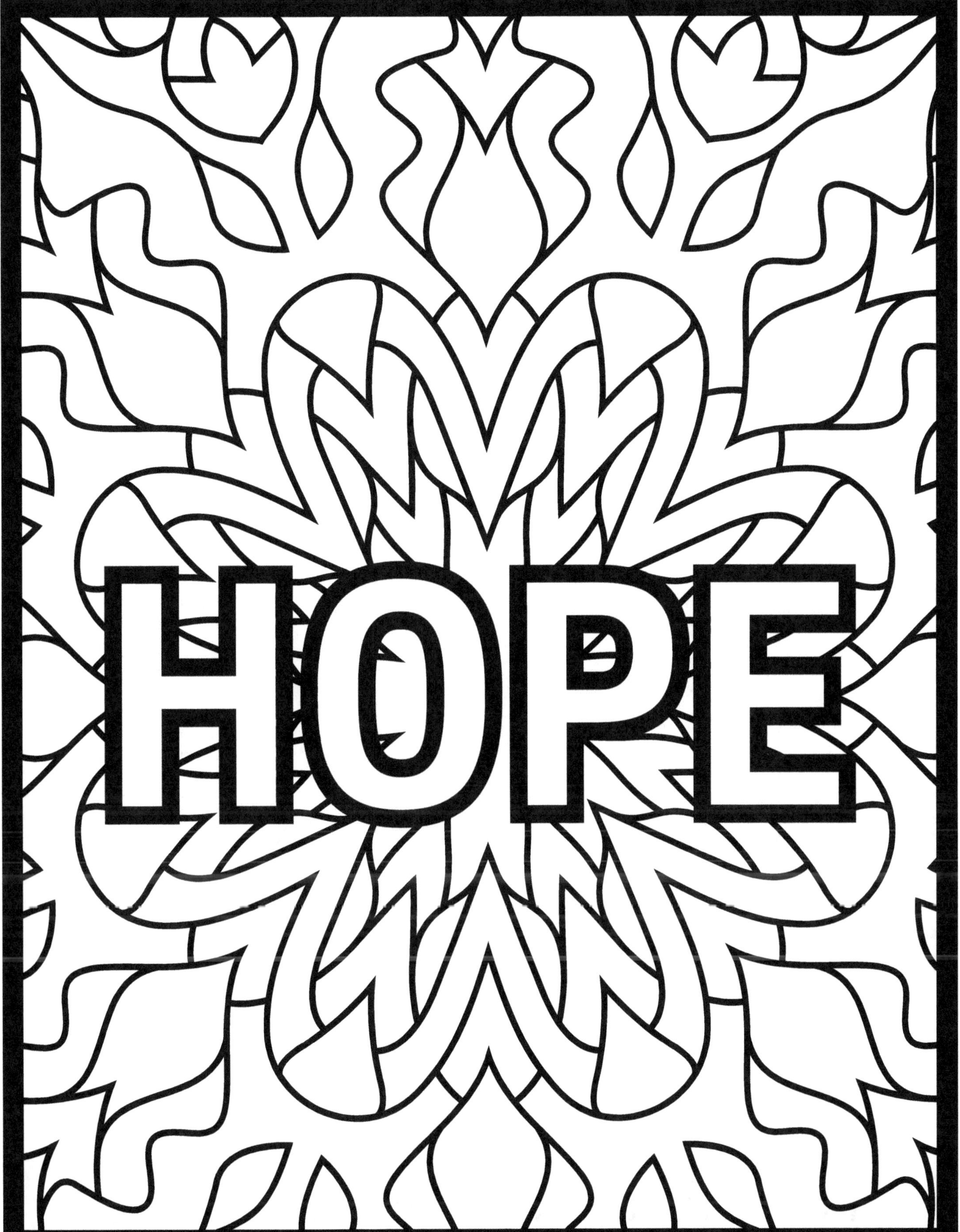

Three things will last forever—faith, hope, and love—and the greatest of these is love. 1 Corinthians 13:13

""Let all that you do be done in love."

1 Corinthians 16:14

GOD HAS A PURPOSE FOR YOUR LIFE! JUST ASK HIM!

GOD HAS A PURPOSE FOR
YOUR LIFE! JUST ASK HIM!

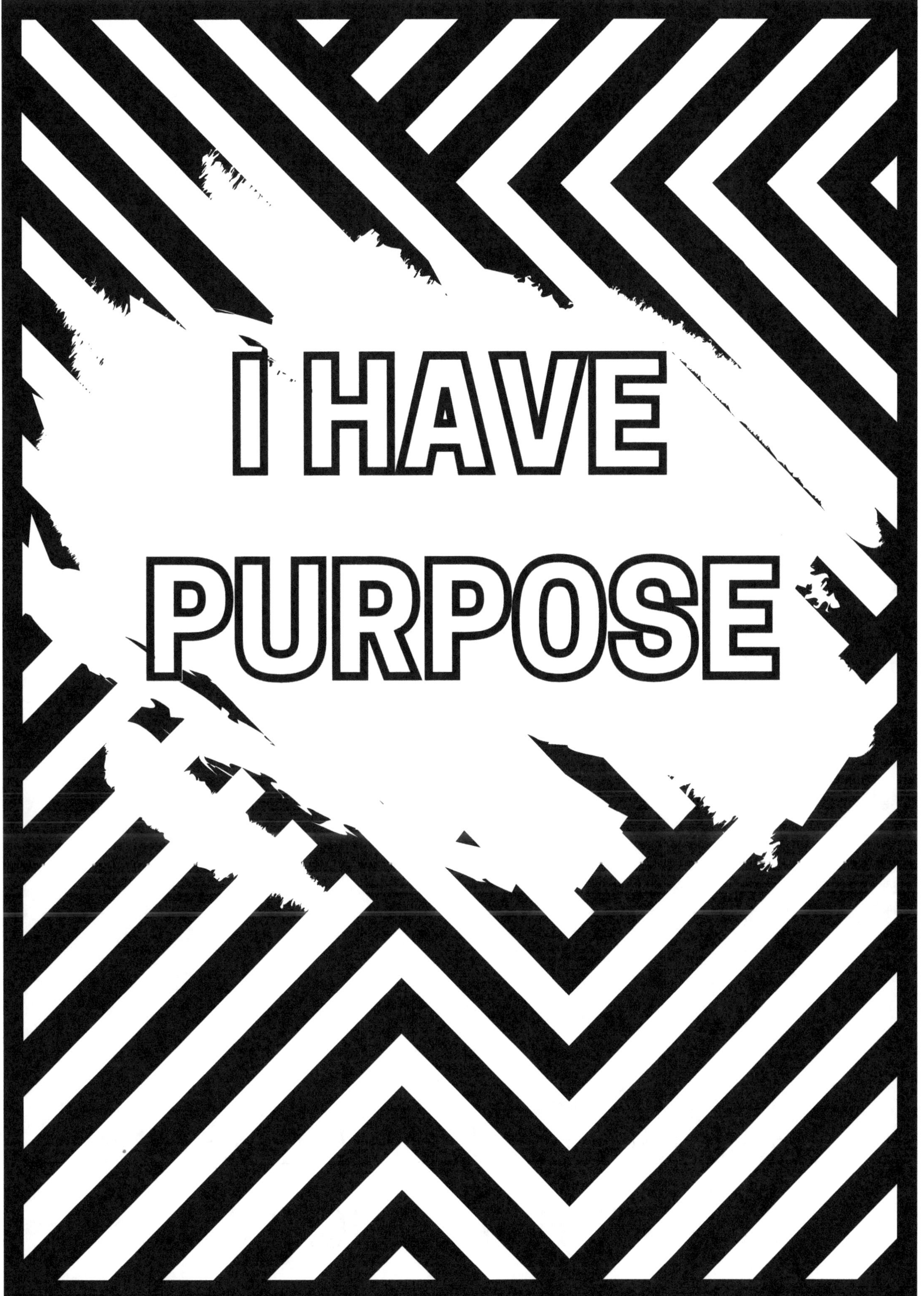
I HAVE
PURPOSE

""Let all that you do be done in love."

1 Corinthians 16:14

CHILD OF A KING!

CHILD OF A KING!

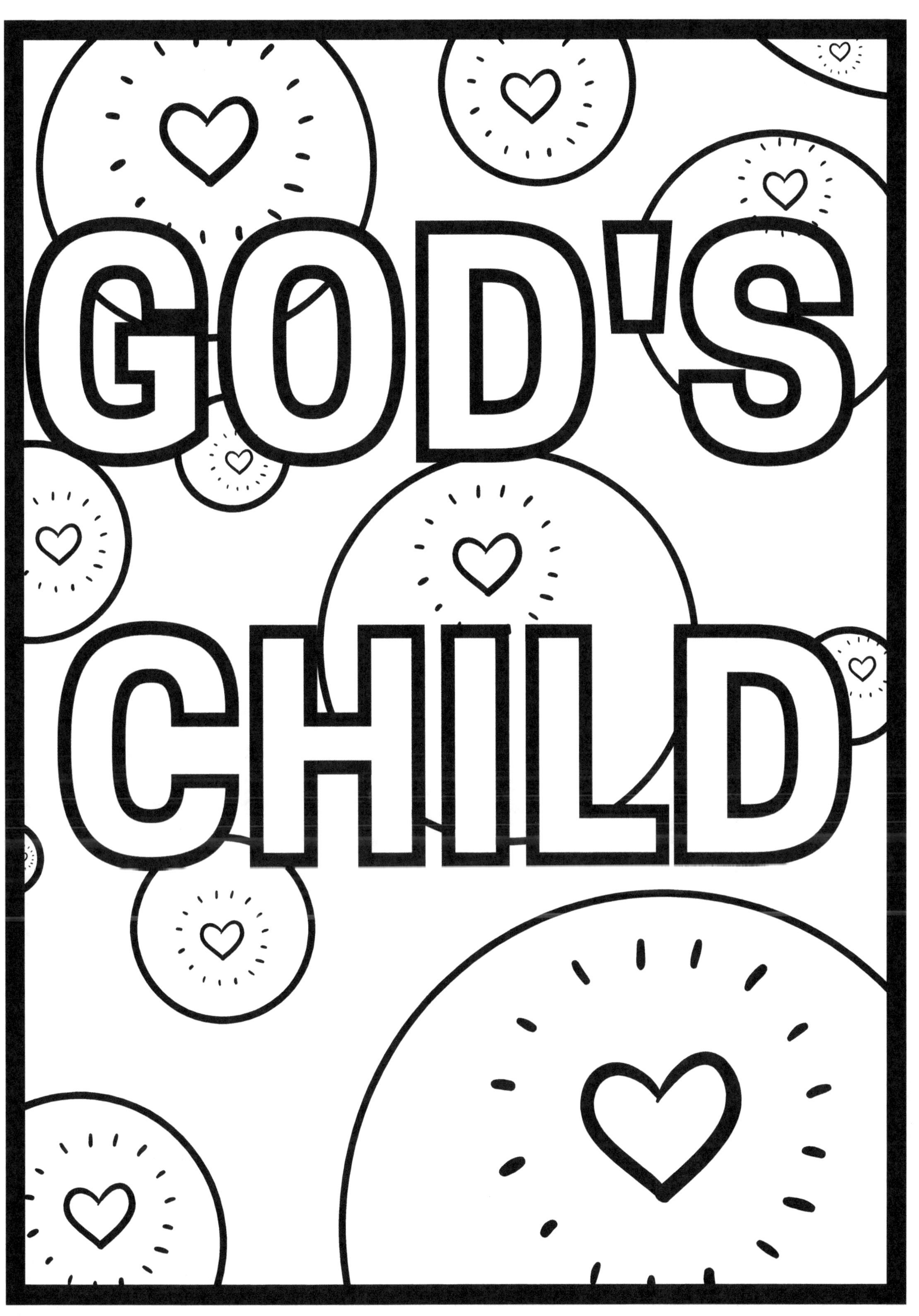
GOD'S
CHILD

""Let all that you do be done in love."

1 Corinthians 16:14

WONDERFULLY MADE!

WONDERFULLY MADE!

I PRAISE YOU BECAUSE I AM FEARFULLY AND WONDERFULLY MADE; YOUR WORKS ARE WONDERFUL, I KNOW THAT FULL WELL.

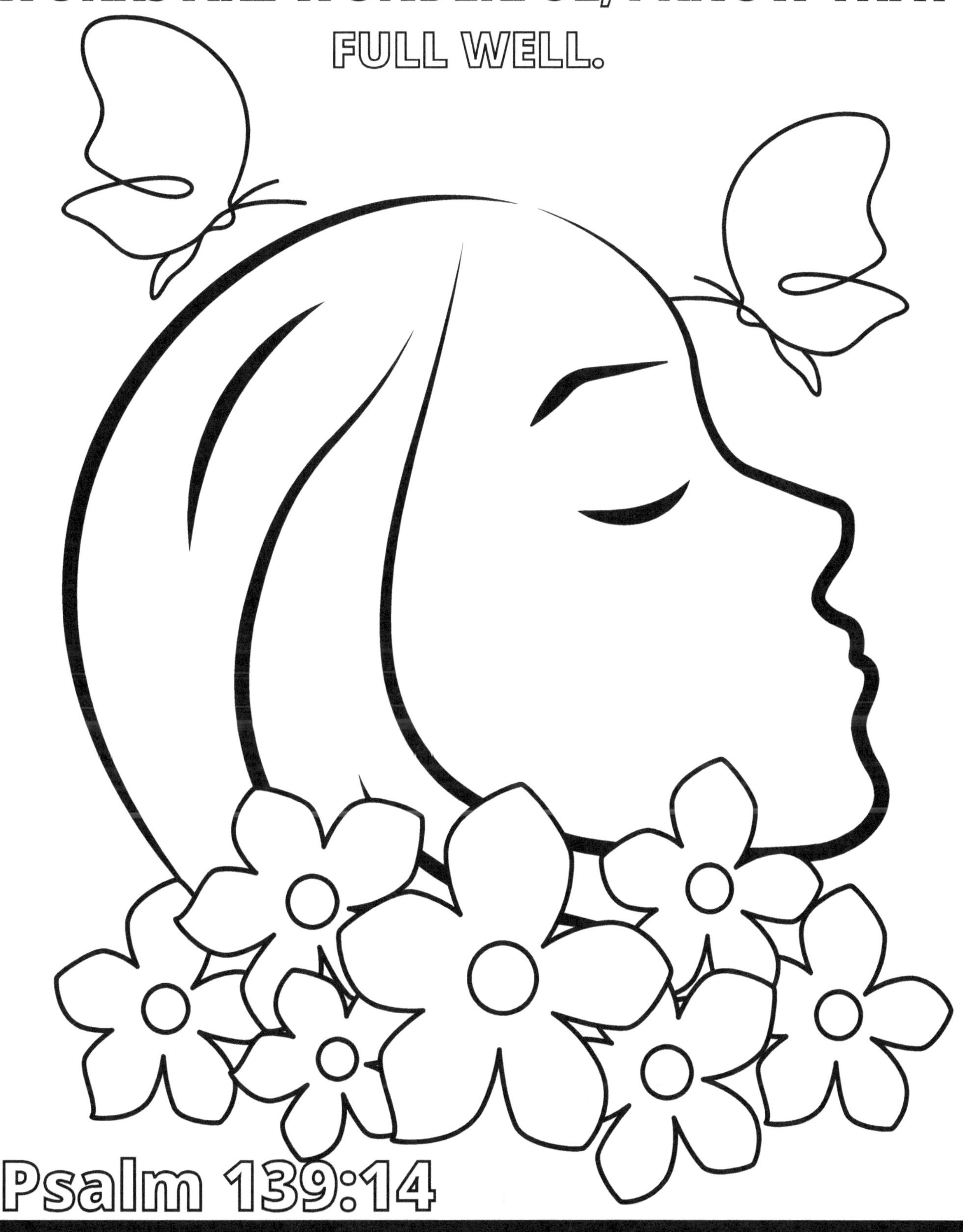

""Let all that you do be done in love."

1 Corinthians 16:14

HEAVEN!

HEAVEN!

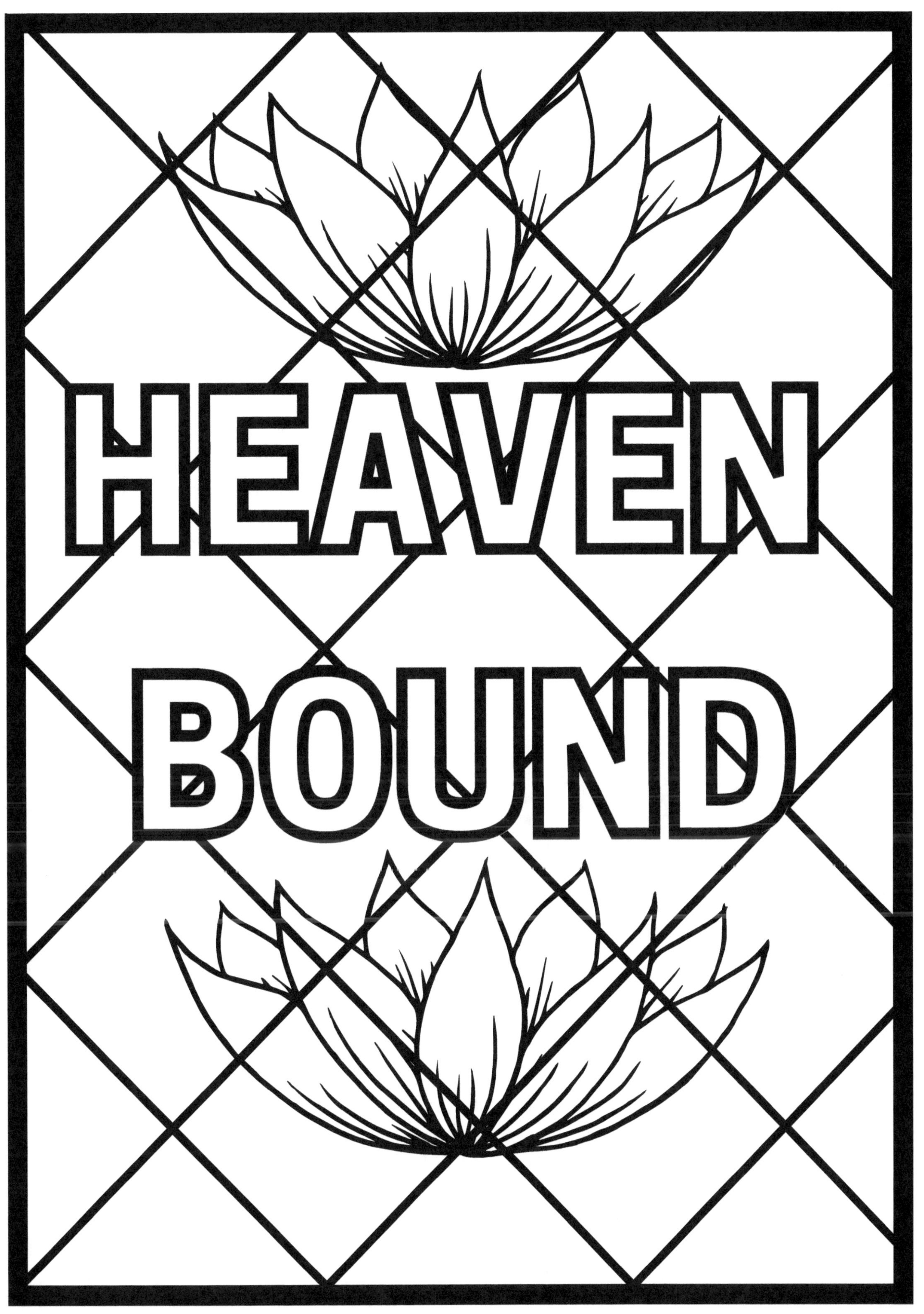
HEAVEN
BOUND

""Let all that you do be done in love."

1 Corinthians 16:14

WITH GOD!

WITH GOD!

JESUS LOOKED
AT THEM AND
SAID, "WITH MAN
THIS IS
IMPOSSIBLE,
BUT WITH GOD
ALL THINGS
ARE POSSIBLE."
MATTHEW 19:26

""Let all that you do be done in love."

1 Corinthians 16:14

JOY!

JOY!

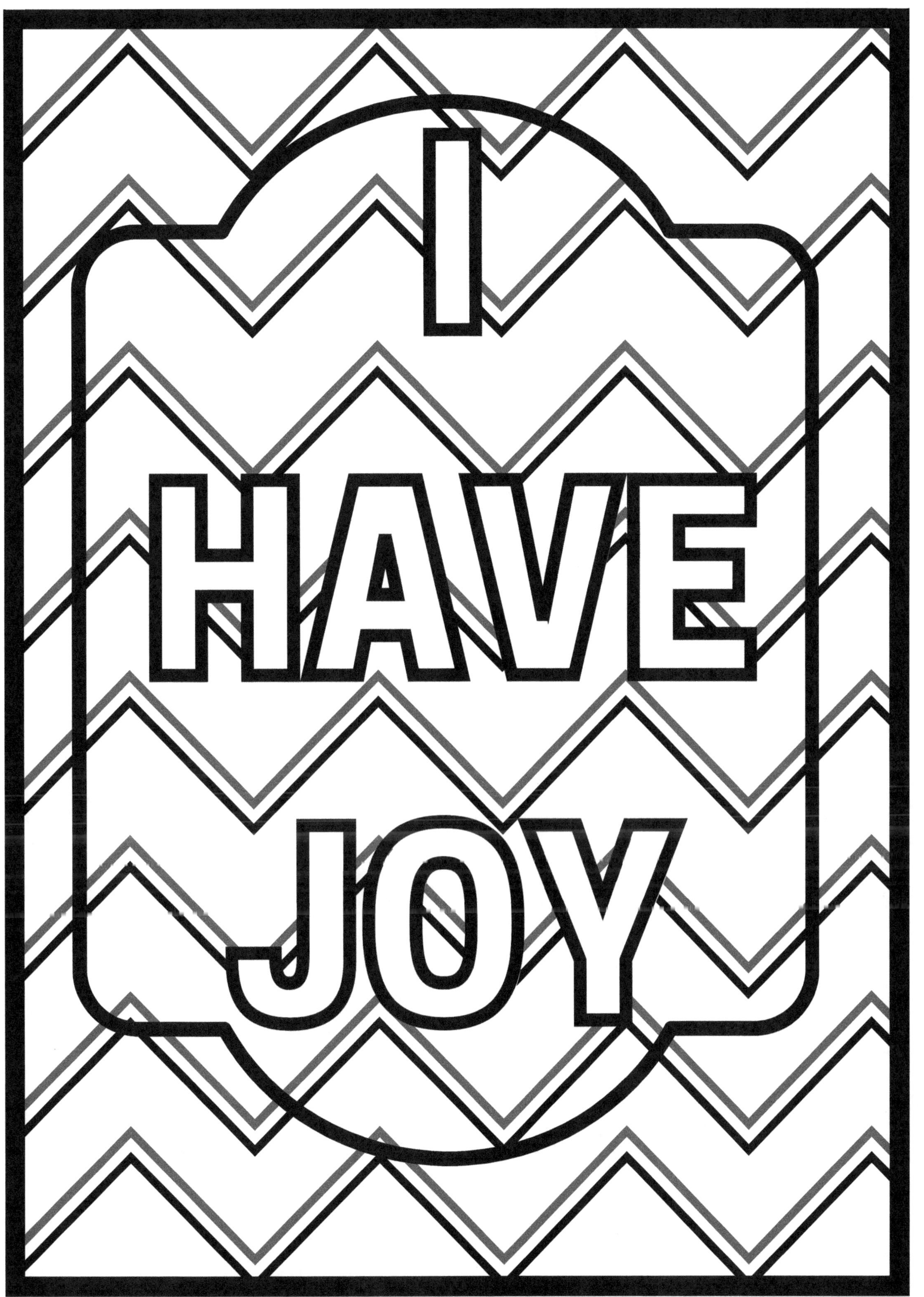
I
HAVE
JOY

""Let all that you do be done in love."

1 Corinthians 16:14

IT'S POSSIBLE!

IT'S POSSIBLE!

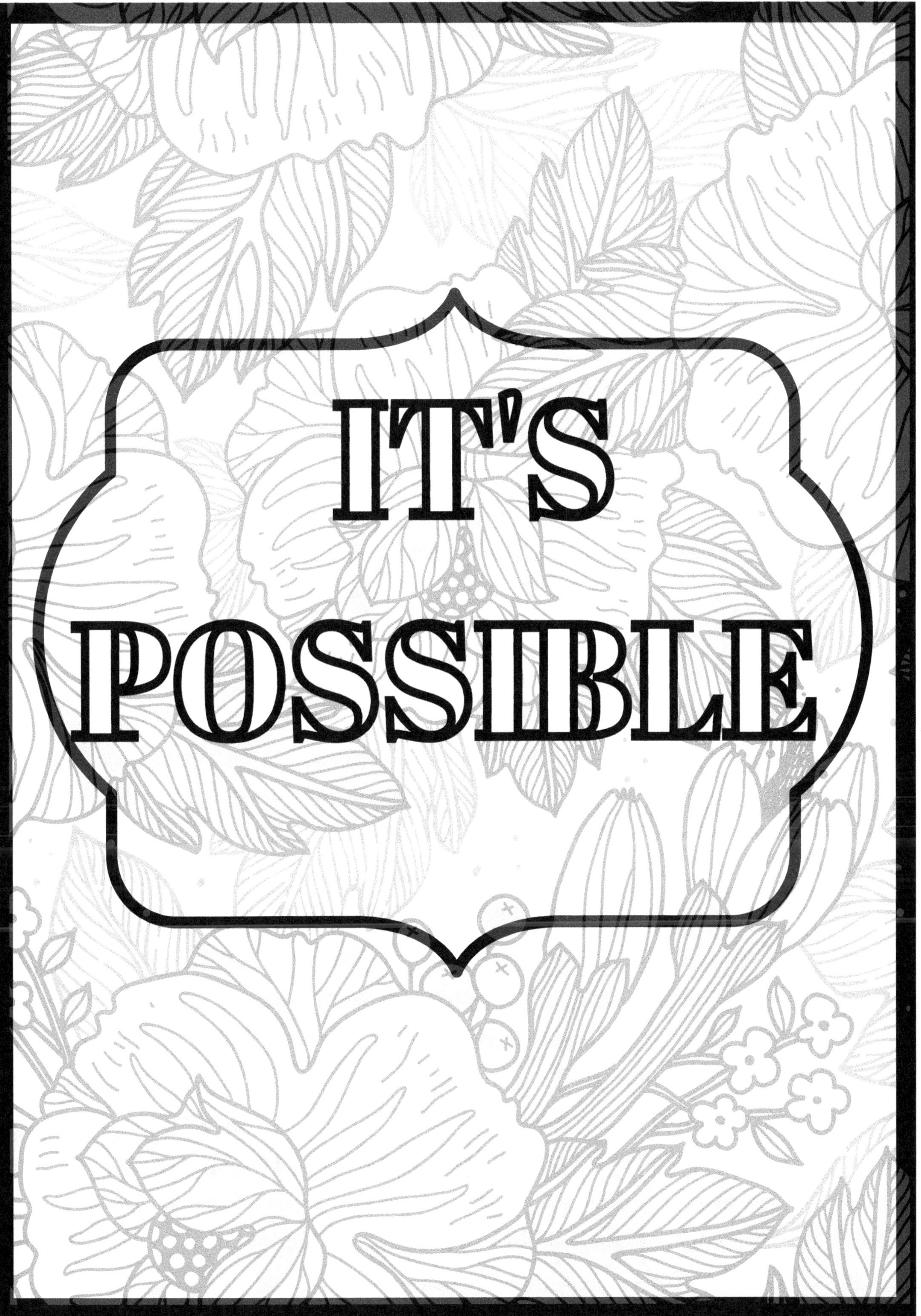
IT'S
POSSIBLE

""Let all that you do be done in love."

1 Corinthians 16:14

JESUS LOVES YOU!

JESUS LOVES YOU!

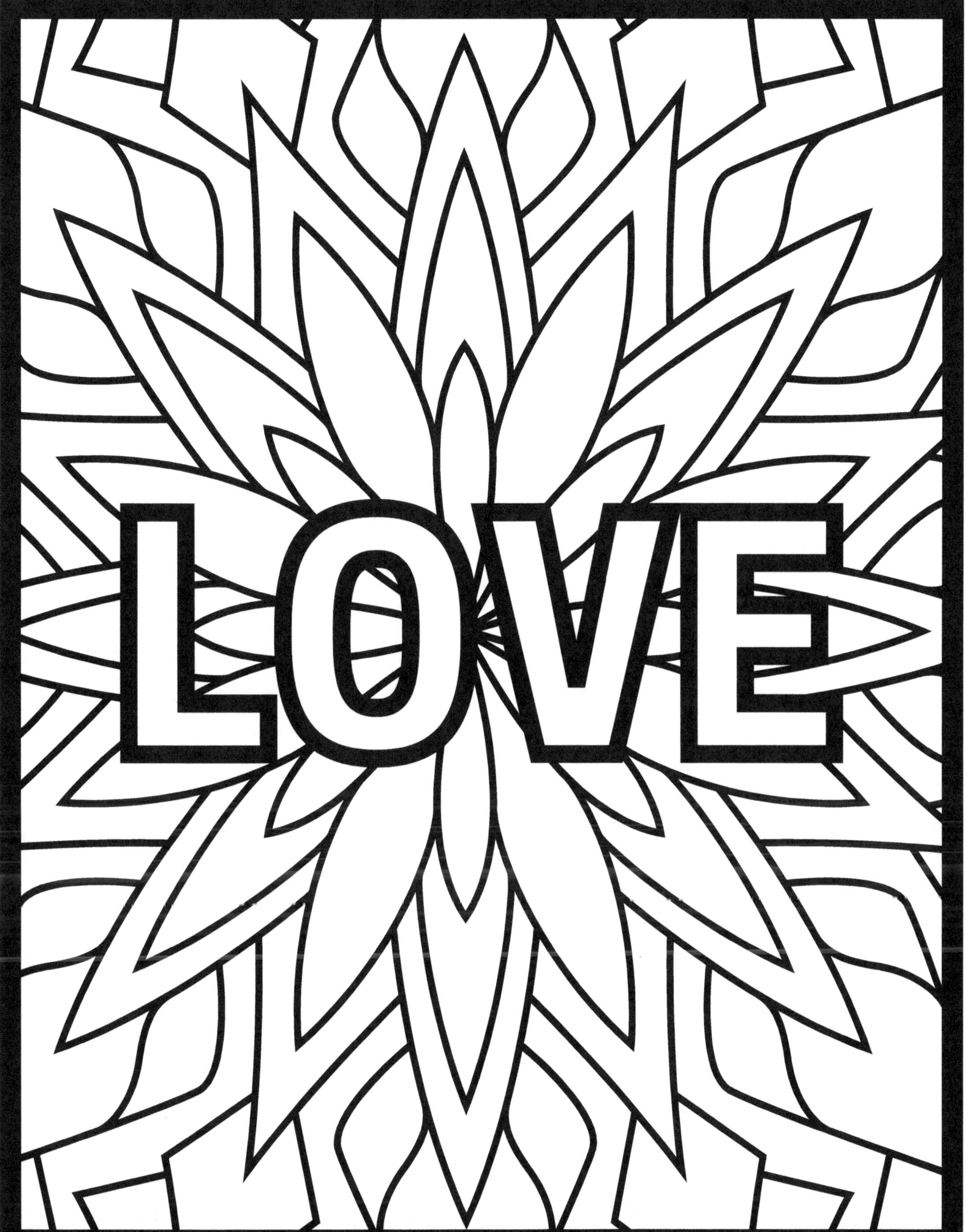

Three things will last forever—faith, hope, and love—and the greatest of these is love. 1 Corinthians 13:13

""Let all that you do be done in love."

1 Corinthians 16:14

www.ingramcontent.com/pod-product-compliance
Lightning Source LLC
LaVergne TN
LVHW061252100826
845148LV00008B/1101
* 9 7 8 1 7 3 7 4 2 6 0 1 1 *